Picture credits: Cover picture: Maria Teresa Meloni; Title page: Joan Freestone, "Stray"; Archiv Fur Kunst: 48 Steinlein, "Die Katz"; Bridgeman Art Library: 5, 14-5 Ditz, "Winter pigs", 17 Ditz, "The Carpet Cat", 18, 21, Willis, "Cat on a Chair", 23 Marek, "On the Mat", 24-5 Smart, "Rooftops in Marakesh", 27 Ditz, "Cat-spread", 31 Page, "Tom, Dick and Henry", 33 Ditz "The Rocking Chair", 38 Page "Punch and Judy", 51 Ditz, "Ivy", 56-7 Honnef, "Kittens Playing" (detail), 59 Page, "Mirror Twins", 61 Ditz, "Fowl and the Pussycat" (detail); Christie's Colour Library: 8, 44-5, 47 Liljefors, "Rap and Johann", 54; e.t. archive: 43 Fred Aris, "Black Cat"; Fine Art Photo Library: 11; Giraudon: 7 Renoir, "Julie Manet"; Mary Evans Picture Library: 13, 35, 41, 53.

Other Cat books by Exley:
The Cat Notebook
The Illustrated Cat Address Book
The Crazy World of Cats
Fanatics Guide to Cats
Cats and Other Crazy Cuddlies

Other books in this series:
Golf Quotations
Horse Quotations
Love Quotations
Teddy Bear Quotations

Published simultaneously in 1992 by Exley Publications Ltd in Great Britain, and Exley Giftbooks in the USA.
First published in Great Britain in 1991 by Exley Publications Ltd
Copyright © Helen Exley 1991
Reprinted 1991, 1992 (five times), 1993 (twice), Ninth printing 1994, Tenth printing 1995
ISBN 1-85015-082-6
A copy of the CIP data is available from the British Library on request.
Designed by Pinpoint Design Company.
Series Editor: Helen Exley
Edited by: Samantha Armstrong
Picture Editor: Alexander Goldberg
Printed by Kossuth Printing House Co. in Hungary.
Exley Publications Ltd, 16 Chalk Hill, Watford, Herts WD1 4BN, United Kingdom.
Exley Giftbooks, 232 Madison Avenue, Suite 1206, NY 10016, USA.

CAT
QUOTATIONS

A COLLECTION OF
LOVABLE CAT PICTURES AND
THE BEST CAT QUOTES

— ◆ —

EXLEY
NEW YORK • WATFORD, UK

"The cat has been described as the most perfect animal, the acme of muscular perfection and the supreme example in the animal kingdom of the co-ordination of mind and muscle."

ROSEANNE AMBROSE-BROWN

– ♦ –

"Poets generally love cats - because poets have no delusions about their own superiority."

MARION GARRETTY

– ♦ –

"Everything a cat is and does physically is to me beautiful, lovely, stimulating, soothing, attractive and an enchantment."

PAUL GALLICO
from *"An Honourable Cat"*

– ♦ –

"I think one reason we admire cats, those of us who do, is their proficiency in one-upmanship. They always seem to come out on top, no matter what they are doing – or pretend to do. Rarely do you see a cat discomfited. They have no conscience, and they never regret. Maybe we secretly envy them."

BARBARA WEBSTER
from *"Creatures and Contentments"*

"Most cats, when they are Out want to be In,
and vice versa, and often simultaneously."

Dr. LOUIS J. CAMUTI

"Any cat who misses a mouse pretends it was
aiming for the dead leaf."

CHARLOTTE GRAY

"If your cat falls out of a tree,
go indoors to laugh."

PATRICIA HITCHCOCK

"They come to sit on the table by the writer, keeping his thoughts company, and gazing at him with intelligent tenderness and magical penetration. It seems as though cats divine the thought that is passing from the brain to the pen, and that as they stretch out a paw, they are trying to seize it on its way."

THEOPHILE GAUTIER
in his memoirs of Beaudelaire

"He loved books and when he found one open on the table he would lie down on it, turn over the edges of the leaves with his paw, and after a while, fall asleep, for all the world as if he had been reading a fashionable novel."

THEOPHILE GAUTIER

French novelist Colette was a firm cat-lover. When she was in the U.S. she saw a cat sitting in the street. She went over to talk to it and the two of them mewed at each other for a friendly minute. Colette turned to her companion and exclaimed, "Enfin! Quelqu'un qui parle francais."

(At last! Someone who speaks French!)

ANON

"Cats only assume their strangest, most intriguing and most beautiful postures when it is impossible to photograph them. Cat calendars always disappoint for they only show the public range of cat positions."

J. R. COULSON

"But the quiet life, fundamentally, is not too interesting for a cat. The idea of a cat satisfied with a saucer of milk and a place by the fire is only half the picture.
The more important half we can only guess at. It starts where we leave off - in the larger community outdoors."

LLOYD ALEXANDER

" A cat is a Regency gentleman – elegant of pose, exquisite of manner, with spotless linen and an enthusiasm for bare knuckle fights, rampaging love affairs, duels by moonlight and the singing of glees. He expects immaculate service from his domestic staff, and possesses a range of invective that would make a navvy blanch."

PAM BROWN

"A cat isn't fussy – just so long as you remember he likes his milk in the shallow, rose-patterned saucer and his fish on the blue plate. From which he will take it, and eat it off the floor."

ARTHUR BRIDGES
Writer and humorist

– ◆ –

"Kittens are wide-eyed, soft and sweet.
With needles in their jaws and feet."

PAM BROWN

"We tie bright ribbons around their necks, and
occasionally little tinkling bells, and we affect to
think that they are as sweet and vapid as the coy
name 'kitty' by which we call them would imply.
It is a curious illusion. For, purring beside our
fireplaces and pattering along our back fences,
we have got a wild beast as uncowed and
uncorrupted as any under heaven."

ALAN DEVOE

"It is a very inconvenient habit of kittens (Alice
had once made the remark) that whatever you
say to them, they *always* purr."

LEWIS CARROLL

"I saw the most beautiful cat today. It was sitting by the side of the road, its two front feet neatly and graciously together. Then it gravely swished around its tail to completely and snugly encircle itself. It was so fit and beautifully neat, that gesture, and so self-satisfied - so complacent."

MARY MORROW LINDBERGH

"One small cat changes coming home to an empty house to coming home."

PAM BROWN

"Cats do not wear their hearts on their sleeves, which is not to say that they do not miss you when you are away. However, they feel that you have behaved very badly and may not be very civil when you return. After you have apologized, normal relations can be resumed."

SUSANNE MILLEN

"A cat who has taken umbrage is a terrible sight to see."

ROSEMARY NISBET

"Cats can be very funny, and have the oddest ways of showing they're glad to see you. Rudimace always peed in our shoes."

W. H. AUDEN

"Dogs come when they are called; cats take a message and get back to you."

MARY BLY

"The really great thing about cats is their endless variety. One can pick a cat to fit almost any kind of decor, income, personality, mood. But under the fur, there still lies, essentially unchanged, one of the world's free souls."

ERIC GURNEY

"There are no ordinary cats."

COLETTE

"To some blind souls all cats are much alike. To a cat lover every cat from the beginning of time has been utterly and amazingly unique."

JENNY DE VRIES

"He makes himself the companion of your hours of solitude, melancholy and toil. He remains for whole evenings on your knee, uttering his contented purr, happy to be with you, and forsaking the company of animals of his own species."

THEOPHILE GAUTIER

— ◆ —

"Only cat lovers know the luxury of fur-coated, musical hot water bottles that never go cold."

SUSANNE MILLEN

— ◆ —

"There are people who reshape the world by force or argument, but the cat just lies there, dozing, and the world quietly reshapes itself to suit his comfort and convenience."

ALLEN *and* IVY DODD

— ◆ —

"A well kept cat has fur as soft and as smooth as silk. Cats' eyes are pools of beauty and enchantment, and the way their oval pupils get smaller and bigger is just wonderful to watch."

SHEILA CONNELL, 13

– ◆ –

"Some of the best five minutes of my life have been spent sitting on garden walls sharing bags of popcorn with newly-made feline acquaintances."

PAM BROWN

"Even overweight cats instinctively know the cardinal rule: when fat, arrange yourself in slim poses."

JOHN WEITZ
American clothes designer

"At dinner time he would sit in a corner, concentrating, and suddenly they would say, 'Time to feed the cat,' as if it was their own idea."

LILIAN JACKSON BRAUN

"Places to look: behind the books in the bookshelf, any cupboard with a gap too small for any cat to squeeze through, the top of anything sheer, under anything too low for a cat to squash under and inside the piano."

ROSEANNE AMBROSE-BROWN

"One cat is fine. She will probably sleep over the hot water bottle, or in the crook of your knees or on your lap or folded in your arms, though there are eccentrics who prefer to wedge themselves under the chin, curl around the head, squat on the hip or ribcage or shoulders or simply insist on lying nose to nose, breathing kipper."

ROSEMARY NISBET

— ◆ —

"A cat can maintain a position of curled up somnolence on your knee until you are nearly upright. To the last minute she hopes your conscience will get the better of you and you will settle down again."

PAM BROWN

— ◆ —

"Cats like doors left open - in case they change their minds."

ROSEMARY NISBET

"Many a cat can only be lured in by switching off all the lights and keeping very still. Until the indignant cry of a cat-locked-out comes at the door."

PAM BROWN

"I love in the cat that independent and most ungrateful temper which prevents it from attaching itself to anyone; the indifference with which it passes from the salon to the housetop."

FRANCOIS RENE DE CHATEAUBRIAND

"A wanderer himself, he is full of reproaches if I am gone beyond the expected time, yet plays with my anxieties when he is late, drifting slowly out of the darkness as if he cannot hear my calling."

SAMANTHA ARMSTRONG

"For me, one of the pleasures of cats' company is their devotion to bodily comfort."

COMPTON MACKENZIE

"The trouble with sharing one's bed with cats is that they'd rather sleep on you than beside you."

PAM BROWN

"A cat refuses to be the object of sentimentality - if she doesn't want to be cuddled, that's it."

SAMANTHA ARMSTRONG

"A cat allows you to sleep on the bed. On the edge."

JENNY DE VRIES

"There are other ties which cats put on our affections. We enjoy their intelligence and grace; and we feel a strange sense of companionship and consolation in their presence. But these are ideas we can understand by words. The reasons for their appeal to us can never be expressed too clearly."

LLOYD ALEXANDER

"We know that Dr. Johnson's cat was called Hodge and that Dr. Johnson loved him dearly. But we have no idea at all what sort of cat Hodge was: whether long-haired or short-haired, whether black or white or yellow. We do not know because that is not important. What was important was that Hodge was a nice cat."

MARION GARRETTY

"All cats like being the focus of attention."

PETER GRAY

– ◆ –

"When I play with my cat, who knows if I am
not a pastime to her more than
she is to me?"

MICHEL E. DE MONTAIGNE

"People meeting for the first time suddenly
relax if they find they both have cats.
And plunge into anecdote."

CHARLOTTE GRAY

"Nobody who is not prepared to spoil cats will
get from them the reward they are able to give
to those who do spoil them."

COMPTON MACKENZIE

"One day a cat will opt to join you while you are utterly relaxed in muscle and brain, and with a delicate miaow and a velvet paw will show you transcendental meditation by an expert."

V. MARTIN

— ♦ —

"After scolding one's cat one looks into its face and is seized by the ugly suspicion that it understood every word.
And has filed it for reference."

CHARLOTTE GRAY

— ♦ —

"There is nothing so lowering to one's self-esteem as the affectionate contempt of a beloved cat."

MONICA EDWARDS

— ♦ —

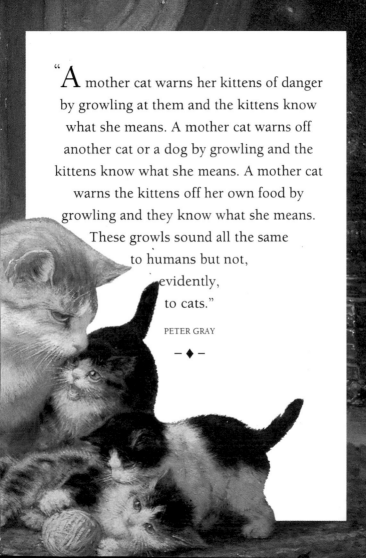

"A mother cat warns her kittens of danger by growling at them and the kittens know what she means. A mother cat warns off another cat or a dog by growling and the kittens know what she means. A mother cat warns the kittens off her own food by growling and they know what she means. These growls sound all the same to humans but not, evidently, to cats."

PETER GRAY

— ◆ —

"A dog will flatter you
but you have to flatter the cat."

GEORGE MIKES
from *"How to be decadent"*

"You can keep a dog; but it is the cat who
keeps people, because cats find humans useful
domestic animals."

GEORGE MIKES
from *"How to be decadent"*

"You own a dog but you feed a cat."

JENNY DE VRIES

— ◆ —

"One is never sure, watching two cats washing each other, whether it's affection, the taste or a trial run for the jugular."

HELEN THOMSON

— ◆ —

"Cats know how to obtain food without labour, shelter without confinement and love without penalties."

W. L. GEORGE

— ♦ —

"A cat sees no good reason why it should obey another animal, even if it does stand on two legs."

SARAH THOMPSON

— ♦ —

"Cats are kindly masters, just so long as you remember your place."

PAUL GRAY

— ♦ —

"Tobermory looked squarely at her for a moment and then fixed his gaze serenely on the middle distance. It was obvious that boring questions like that lay outside his scheme of life."

SAKI

— ◆ —

"Cats have very sad faces. They look at you a long time and think about you.
They are peaceful to have around."

A YOUNG CHILD

— ◆ —

"A cat does not want all the world to love her - only those she has chosen to love."

HELEN THOMSON

"It is a well-known fact that the survival rate after heart-attacks is significantly higher among pet-owners than non-owners, and that human blood pressure falls in the presence of companion animals - especially cats."

Dr. MAYA PATEL

"If you are worthy of its affection, a cat will be your friend, but never your slave."

THEOPHILE GAUTIER

"One must love a cat on its own terms."

PETER GRAY

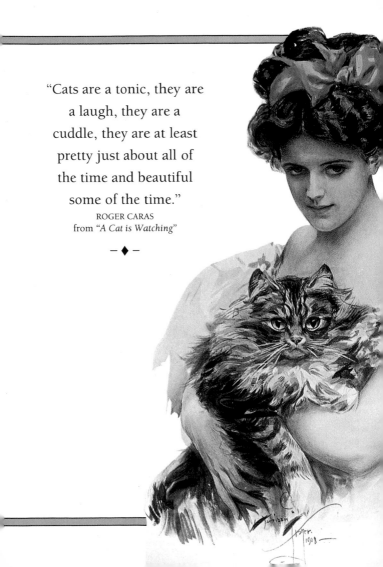

"Cats are a tonic, they are
a laugh, they are a
cuddle, they are at least
pretty just about all of
the time and beautiful
some of the time."

ROGER CARAS
from *"A Cat is Watching"*

– ◆ –

"Cats can work out mathematically the
exact place to sit that will cause
most inconvenience."

PAM BROWN

"Most cats enjoy kneading - digging their
claws into rugs, fabrics or human
arms or legs.
It exercises certain muscles,
but I think they do it for fun, too."

LLOYD ALEXANDER

"Cats have an infallible understanding of total
concentration - and get between you and it."

ARTHUR BRIDGES

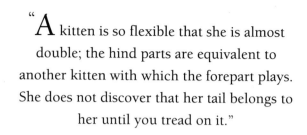

"A kitten is so flexible that she is almost double; the hind parts are equivalent to another kitten with which the forepart plays. She does not discover that her tail belongs to her until you tread on it."

HENRY DAVID THOREAU

— ◆ —

"I wish you could see the two cats drowsing side by side in a Victorian nursing chair, their paws, their ears, their tails complementally adjusted, their blue eyes blinking open on a single thought of when I shall remember it's their suppertime. They might have been composed by Bach for two flutes."

SYLVIA TOWNSEND WARNER

"There were pots of geraniums on the high window sill, with a tortoiseshell cat curled up between them where the sun made a splash. Cyril went across and stroked it – he was always fond of cats – and it got up, stretched itself, arched its back and purred. The clock ticked on slowly, and there was a faint buzzing of bees. It seemed as if nothing wanted to wake up."

ERNEST H. SHEPHARD,
from *"Dawn from Memory"*

Desold Page 1981

"If a man could be crossed with a cat, it would improve man but it would deteriorate the cat."

MARK TWAIN

"If the pull of the outside world is strong, there is also a pull towards the human. The cat may disappear on its own errands, but sooner or later, it returns once again for a little while, to greet us with its own type of love. Independent as they are, cats find more than pleasure in our company."

LLOYD ALEXANDER

"Cats were put into the world to disprove the dogma that all things were created to serve man."

PAUL GRAY

"Cat said, 'I am not a friend, and I am not a Servant. I am the Cat who walks by himself, and I wish to come into your Cave.'"

RUDYARD KIPLING
from the *"Just-So Stories"*

— ◆ —